The Holocaust

Sean Sheehan

W
FRANKLIN WATTS
LONDON•SYDNEY

First published in 2007 by Franklin Watts

Copyright © 2007 Arcturus Publishing Limited

Franklin Watts
338 Euston Road
London NW1 3BH

Franklin Watts Australia
Level 17/207 Kent Street, Sydney, NSW 2000

Produced by Arcturus Publishing Limited,
26/27 Bickels Yard, 151–153 Bermondsey Street, London SE1 3HA

The right of Sean Sheehan to be identified as the author of this work has been asserted by him in accordance with the Copyright, Designs and Patents Act 1988.

Series concept: Alex Woolf
Project manager and editor: Liz Miles
Designer: Simon Borrough
Picture researcher: Liz Miles
Consultant: James Vaughan
Cartographer: LMS

Picture credits:
Corbis: cover (dpa/Corbis), 5, 6 (Hulton-Deutsch Collection/Corbis), 7 (Bettmann/Corbis), 8, 9 (Corbis), 10 (Hulton-Deutsch Collection/Corbis), 11, 12, 13, 16, 18 (Bettmann/Corbis), 19 (David Sutherland/Corbis), 20 (Antoine Gyori/Corbis Sygma), 21, 22 (Bettmann/Corbis), 23 (Michael St. Maur Sheil/Corbis), 24, 25 (Bettmann/Corbis), 26 (The Dmitri Baltermants Collection/Corbis), 28, 29 (Hulton-Deutsch Collection/Corbis), 31 (Franz-Marc Frei/Corbis), 32 (Bettmann/Corbis), 33 (Yevgeny Khaldei/Corbis), 35 (Bettmann/Corbis), 36 (Yevgeny Khaldei/Corbis), 38 (Ira Nowinski/Corbis), 39 (Michael St. Maur Sheil/Corbis), 40 (Hulton-Deutsch Collection/Corbis), 41 (Corbis), 42 (Bettmann/Corbis), 43 (Corbis), 44 (Howard Davies/Corbis), 45 (Greene Jeff/Corbis).
TopFoto: 4, 14 (TopFoto/HIP), 27 (2004 Roger-Viollet/TopFoto), 30 (TopFoto/HIP), 34, 37 (Topham Picturepoint).
Rex Features: 15 (Tim Rooke).

Every attempt has been made to clear copyright. Should there be any inadvertent omission, please apply to the publisher for rectification.

A CIP catalogue record for this book is available from the British Library.

Dewey Decimal Classification Number: 940.53'18

ISBN 978 0 7496 7189 1

Printed in China

Franklin Watts is a division of Hachette Children's Books.

Contents

Protocols of the Elders of Zion First Published

The Protocols of the Elders of Zion is a book about how a group of Jews, the Elders, are planning to take over the world. The book describes how these Elders secretly meet to discuss how they will achieve control of the world and destroy the existing order of society. The whole book appeared in 1905, two years after parts of it were first published in a Russian newspaper, and translations into many languages made it well known around the world.

IMPACT OF *THE PROTOCOLS*

The Protocols of the Elders of Zion, however, was proved to be a complete forgery. Despite this, the book became enormously popular and in Germany it became a way of explaining the country's defeat in World War I. Many people wanted to believe in the idea of a Jewish conspiracy because it fitted in with their prejudice against Jews.

ANTI-SEMITISM

There were thousands of Jewish communities, especially in Eastern Europe, where Jews had lived for over two thousand years and practised their own religion, Judaism. Christianity was not kind to Judaism, and Jews were persecuted through the ages as a minority group. Violent attacks, known as pogroms, were made on Jewish communities in Russia and France towards the end of the nineteenth century.

Prejudice against Jews, called anti-Semitism, further developed in many European countries in the 1920s and 1930s. In these decades, in Poland, Romania, Latvia, Lithuania and Greece, laws discriminating against Jews were passed. In many European countries it was not unusual to limit the number of Jews who could attend university. In Germany, Jews were accused of weakening the country and in 1920 a politician called Adolf Hitler said that no Jew should be a German citizen. Hitler was born in Austria and he grew up in a climate of anti-Semitism, hearing extremist politicians warning of the 'Jewish peril'.

Jewish men examine the damage done to Torah scrolls, sacred religious texts, during pogroms in 1881 in Russia.

| TIMELINE | THE GROWTH OF ANTI-SEMITISM 1881–1923 |

1881–82 ▶	Pogroms in Russia.
28 August 1903 ▶	*The Protocols of the Elders of Zion* first published in a Russian newspaper.
15 February 1919 ▶	1,700 Jews murdered in a pogrom in the Ukraine; by the end of 1919 around 60,000 Jews have died at the hands of anti-Semitic gangs.
1920 ▶	First German translation of *The Protocols of the Elders of Zion*.
1921 ▶	The book is proved to be a forgery.
24 June 1922 ▶	Walter Rathenau, a Jew who had been Germany's foreign minister, is murdered by anti-Semites; Hitler expresses pleasure at the assassination.
16–30 October 1923 ▶	Around 70 Jews are expelled from Bavaria, a province in Germany bordering with Austria.

The victims of a Jewish pogrom in Russia, a country where such pogroms were common from 1871 onwards.

CROSS-REFERENCE
RISE OF HITLER:
PAGES 6–7
POGROMS: PAGES
10–11, 12–13

The Protocols in Germany

Although *The Protocols of the Elders of Zion* was proved to be a forgery, millions of copies were sold and in Germany alone over 30 editions of the book appeared in the 1920s and 1930s. Hitler read the book and claimed it was not a forgery but a true account of the danger represented by Jewish people and their way of life. The book encouraged anti-Semitic ideas and helped allow some people to think that Hitler was right in blaming Jews for the poor state of the country.

Even today, the book is still published in some countries and used to support anti-Semitism.

Hitler Appointed Chancellor of Germany

30 JANUARY 1933

Hitler was an unknown politician when he became leader of the German Nazi party in 1920. Although at the time the party had only 60 members, its popularity gradually increased by appealing to people's fears. Millions of people were unemployed in the cities, and farmers were finding it difficult to make a good living. There was no strong government in Germany but many political parties, and people became fed up with the arguing that went on between them. Lots of working people supported communist parties and this scared middle-class and rich people who feared they would lose out if there was a communist government.

Adolf Hitler, on the left, shakes hands with the President of Germany after being appointed chancellor of the country.

HITLER'S APPEAL

The Nazi party promised to make Germany a strong nation again. Hitler spoke about the purity of German blood, and Jews were labelled as impure outsiders. Communists were also attacked and for many people this increased the appeal of the Nazis. Hitler hated Jews, as did many of his supporters, but he did not always make too much of this because he wanted to appear as a sensible politician who could be trusted to run the country.

DEMOCRATIC ELECTIONS

In the first election of 1932, nearly 14 million people out of 45 million voted for the Nazis. This meant that over 30 million people chose not to vote for Hitler, and the Nazis did not have a majority of seats in the country's parliament. In a second election that year, fewer people voted for Hitler. Although the Nazis were the largest party in parliament, Hitler could have been defeated if other parties had joined forces to oppose him. This did not happen and, instead,

CROSS-REFERENCE
NAZI LAWS: PAGES
8–9

anti-communist parties agreed to accept Hitler as chancellor. He took office on 30 January 1933. Within a short while, organized attacks on Jews began in German towns.

Less than two months after Hitler became Germany's leader, parliament gave him the power to pass his own laws. The Nazis were now dictators of Germany and could treat the country's Jews as they wished.

TIMELINE	NAZISM IN GERMANY 1920–1933
8 August 1920	▶ The Nazi party is set up in Germany.
9 November 1923	▶ Hitler fails in an attempt to seize power in Munich.
18 July 1925	▶ First part of *Mein Kampf*, an anti-Semitic book written by Hitler while in prison, is published.
4 July 1926	▶ A youth movement is set up by the Nazi party to recruit young members.
9 March 1933	▶ Anti-Jewish riots break out for the first time in Germany's capital, Berlin.
20 March 1933	▶ First concentration camp is set up, for political prisoners.
30 March 1933	▶ Hitler becomes dictator of Germany.

Thousands of young Germans attend a Nazi rally in Berlin, holding up their right hands in a salute to Hitler.

When Hitler gained power

'I had been skating that day. When I got home we heard that Hitler had become Chancellor. **Everybody shook**. As kids of ten we shook.'

Leslie Frankel remembers how he felt as a ten-year-old Jewish boy on hearing the news. Quoted in Martin Gilbert, *The Holocaust* (Fontana/Collins, 1986).

ELECTIONS IN GERMANY (PERCENTAGE OF VOTES WON BY THE NAZIS)

20 May 1928	2.6%
14 September 1930	18%
31 July 1932	37%
6 November 1932	33%

Nuremberg Laws Passed

The German parliament was based in the capital, Berlin, but in September 1935 it met in the city of Nuremberg and Hitler announced a new set of laws. The first law made the swastika the flag of Germany. The second law declared that Jewish people were no longer citizens of the country, and a third made it illegal for marriages to take place between Germans and Jews. The Nuremberg Laws defined a Jew as anyone with three Jewish grandparents, or with two Jewish grandparents and married to a Jew, or anyone belonging to the Jewish religion.

OTHER LAWS

These were not the first laws directed against Jews. In April 1933, laws had been passed making it impossible for Jews to become teachers or join sporting associations. Other laws had made it illegal for Jews to perform on stage or in films, or for Jewish newspapers to be displayed or sold in public. 'Jews not wanted' signs began to appear above roads leading into towns and villages, and Jews were prevented from visiting cinemas, theatres, swimming pools and seaside resorts.

ATTITUDES TO JEWS

Generally speaking, public opinion was not opposed to the Nazis' anti-Semitic laws and most churches did not protest. Germans, especially communists, who were opposed to Nazism, were arrested and put in special prisons run by the SS. The first of these concentration camps was established at Dachau, near Munich, in 1933.

Jews who could afford to emigrate began to leave Germany but other countries were not always willing to accept them. This became clear in 1938 when foreign governments held a meeting in Evian, France, to discuss

The swastika, which became Germany's new flag, is displayed at a Nazi rally in Nuremberg.

CROSS-REFERENCE
INCREASING ANTI-
SEMITISM: PAGES
10–11
ORGANIZING THE
HOLOCAUST: PAGES
16–17

TIMELINE	ANTI-SEMITIC LAWS 1933–1938
4 April 1933	The German Boxing Association is closed to Jewish boxers.
7 April 1933	First anti-Semitic laws are passed, forcing Jews to retire from government jobs.
27 April 1933	Some 300 people demonstrate against the opening of a Jewish-owned shoe company in the German city of Königsstrasse.
10 May 1933	First mass-burning of books written by Jews.
September 1933	Jews are forbidden to work in agriculture or own farms.
October 1933	Hospitals in Berlin are declared 'free' of all Jewish doctors.
31 December 1933	By the end of 1933, 37,000 of the 525,000 Jews in Germany had left the country.
5 July 1938	Evian Conference.

ways of helping Germany's Jews. No country was prepared to declare that it would open its borders to Jewish refugees. As the number of Jews wishing to leave Germany increased, Britain, the USA and a number of other countries imposed new restrictions on the admission of Jewish refugees.

A Nazi placard, hung outside a Jewish store in Berlin, urges shoppers not to buy anything from Jews.

The SS

The SS was an organization that originally provided personal bodyguards for Hitler. Under the racist Heinrich Himmler, an important Nazi politician, it developed into a special armed force which targeted Jews. By 1933, it had 50,000 members and three years later the members were being told: 'The Jew is a parasite. Wherever he flourishes, the people die ... Elimination of the Jew from our community is to be regarded as an emergency defence measure.' The SS became the main instrument for carrying out the Holocaust.

Quotation from Lucy S. Dawidowics, *The War against the Jews 1933–45* (Penguin, 1987).

Kristallnacht

To the east of Germany lay Poland and when thousands of Polish-born Jews were forced to leave Germany in 1938 they were taken by train to the Polish border. Distressed and mistreated, one of them, who had lived in Germany for nearly thirty years, sent a postcard to his son in Paris. He described how 'the SS men were whipping us, those who lingered they hit and blood was flowing on the road'. The angry son went to the German embassy in Paris and shot an official.

'NIGHT OF THE BROKEN GLASS'

Nazi leaders used the incident in Paris as an excuse to step up the persecution of Germany's Jews. On the night of 9–10 November 1938

Attack on a synagogue

'Men had climbed on to the roof of the synagogue and were hurling the tiles down, others were cutting the cross-beams as soon as they were bare of cover. It did not take long before the first heavy grey stones came tumbling down, and the children of the village amused themselves as they flung stones into the many-coloured windows. When the first rays of a cold and pale November sun penetrated the heavy dark clouds, **the little synagogue was but a heap of stone**, broken glass and smashed-up woodwork.'

This description by Michael Lucas who witnessed an attack on a synagogue helps explain how the pogrom became known as *Kristallnacht*.
Quoted in Dan Cohn-Sherbok, *Understanding the Holocaust* (Cassell, 1999).

This synagogue's Jewish caretaker, and his wife, are thought to have died in an attack when the building was set alight on Kristallnacht.

they organized violent attacks on Jewish homes and burnt down synagogues. During this pogrom, which became known as *Kristallnacht* ('Night of the Broken Glass'), 90 Jews were killed. Nazi leaders pretended it was an unplanned event by ordinary Germans who were outraged by what had happened in Paris.

AFTER *KRISTALLNACHT*

The Nazi persecution of Jews had been increasing since Hitler first came to power and *Kristallnacht* showed the Nazis they could get away with murder. They had also learnt that Jews could be forced to pack their belongings in a suitcase, leave their homes and be taken away in trains. After *Kristallnacht*, 20,000 Jews were rounded up and sent to concentration camps.

Protests against the Nazis took place outside the country, and in the USA newspapers across the country condemned the events of 9–10 November. Despite this, Jewish refugees did not find it any easier to leave Germany and, within Germany, there was little opposition to what was happening.

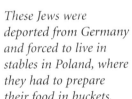

CROSS-REFERENCE ANTI-SEMITIC LAWS LEADING TO *KRISTALLNACHT*: PAGES 8–9

These Jews were deported from Germany and forced to live in stables in Poland, where they had to prepare their food in buckets.

Nazi Invasion of the Soviet Union

Hitler planned to dominate the whole of Europe, and World War II started after the German invasion of Poland. After the invasion, camps were created in the Polish countryside to hold the country's Jewish population. In Polish cities, Jews were forced to live in areas called ghettos. A special force, the *Einsatzgruppen*, was created by the SS to round up Jews.

JEWS IN THE SOVIET UNION

Over a million Jews had fled eastwards from Poland, hoping to find safety in the Soviet Union. While Russia was the largest country in the Soviet Union, there were also smaller countries, like Latvia, Lithuania and Ukraine, where millions of Jews lived. When Germany invaded the Soviet Union on 22 June 1941, all these Jews were at the mercy of Nazism.

THE HOLOCAUST BEGINS

Jews had been terribly mistreated – many were killed and thousands were left to starve to death in the Polish ghettos – but there had been no plans to organize their mass murder. This changed with the invasion of the

Supplies pass by as German troops rest on the roadside during their invasion of the Soviet Union.

Einsatzgruppen

'I turned my eyes towards the man doing the shooting. He was an SS man; he sat, legs swinging, on the edge of the ditch. He had an automatic rifle resting on his knees... The people, completely naked, climbed down steps which had been cut into the clay wall of the ditch, stumbled over the heads of those lying there and stopped at the spot indicated by the SS man. **They lay down on top of the dead or wounded;** some stroked those still living and spoke quietly to them. Then I heard a series of rifle shots. I looked into the ditch and saw the bodies...'

A German, Hermann Grabe, witnessed the *Einsatzgruppen* at work in the Soviet Union. Quoted in Dan Cohn-Sherbok, *Understanding the Holocaust* (Cassell, 1999).

CROSS-REFERENCE
DEPORTATION OF
JEWS: PAGES
20–21, 24–25
AND 26–27

TIMELINE	INVASIONS 1939–1941
March 1939	▶ Germany invades Czechoslovakia.
1 September 1939	▶ Germany invades Poland.
3 September 1939	▶ Start of World War II.
April–June 1940	▶ Germany conquers Denmark, Norway, the Netherlands, Belgium and France.
May 1940	▶ The Dutch surrender and Belgium falls.
14 June 1940	▶ German army enters Paris.
6 April 1941	▶ German invasion of Yugoslavia, where more than 70,000 Jews were living; anti-Semitic groups begin murdering Jews.
28 June 1941	▶ Police in Lithuania begin searching for Jews and more than 200 are beaten to death.

Soviet Union. Four *Einsatzgruppen* units, attached to the regular German army, were ordered to identify and murder Jews. They also encouraged anti-Semitic groups in Latvia, Lithuania, Ukraine and elsewhere to carry out their own massacres. The speed of the German invasion and the organized acts of murder that immediately took place made it very difficult for Jews to escape. The Holocaust – the organized killing of every Jew in Europe – had begun. In the twelve months following the invasion of the Soviet Union, more than one million Jews were murdered.

The body of a man, murdered by Nazis for resisting German rule, is displayed in public in Yugoslavia.

First Death Camp Starts Operating

Sometime around the middle of 1941 (the exact date is not known), Nazi leaders decided on the organized killing of all Jews in Europe. The task of murdering them was given to the *Einsatzgruppen* and by the end of the year about 440,000 Jews had been shot dead. However, it became clear that this method would make it difficult to kill a population numbered in millions. Himmler was ordered to look into other methods of killing, and experiments were carried out using poison gases, including the poisonous exhaust, carbon monoxide, from vehicles.

CHELMNO

Chelmno was a village in Poland, close to the ghetto of Lodz where thousands of Jews had been collected. On 8 December 1941, for the first time, Jews were led into the back of a large van at Chelmno and bottled carbon monoxide was fed into the van to kill the occupants. After a few weeks, the vans were adapted so that pipes from the engine fed the exhaust into the back of the vehicle. By the time the van reached a forest outside Chelmno, the people inside were all dead. The following month a survivor from Chelmno, Michael Podklebnik, witnessed Jews being told at the camp through a loudspeaker: 'Now you are going to the bath-house; you will get new clothes and go to work.'

Chelmno van witness

'At about eleven o'clock the first van loaded with victims arrived... After they had been tossed out of the van two Germans in plain clothes stepped up to them to make a thorough check if anything had been hidden. If they saw a necklace round a throat they tore it off. **They wrenched rings from fingers, and pulled gold teeth out of mouths.**'

Yakov Crojanowski, one of the prisoners held at Chelmno, managed to escape and write this account of what he saw.
Quoted in Martin Gilbert, *The Holocaust* (Fontana/Collins, 1986).

A Jew in a Polish ghetto displaying the Star of David badge that Jews were forced to wear as a mark of their Jewishness.

TIMELINE

FIRST DEATH CAMPS 1941–1942

3 September 1941 ▶ In an experiment using a poison gas 600 Soviet prisoners of war are killed at Auschwitz.

23 October 1941 ▶ All Jews forbidden to leave Nazi-occupied countries.

1 November 1941 ▶ Construction work on Belzec death camp gets underway.

6 January 1942 ▶ Michael Podklebnik, sent to Chelmno to dig pits for those gassed, finds a message scratched on a wall: 'No one leave this place alive.'

22–28 February 1942 ▶ Around 10,000 Jews from the Polish ghetto of Lodz are gassed at Chelmno.

11 March 1942 ▶ The first deportation of Jews from central Europe to Belzec gets underway.

Podklebnik remembered that some of the people began to applaud, happy at the prospect of work.

The gas vans used at Chelmno could each hold around 60 people and in less than a year around 350,000 Jews were murdered. Small groups of Jews were kept as prisoners and forced to do the job of removing and burying the corpses.

Empty cans of Zyklon B from Auschwitz. The gas was used to murder around one million Jews.

ZYKLON B
Another poison gas, cyanide, was found to be effective in killing victims quickly and it did not require vehicle engines. The German trade name of this gas was Zyklon B and plans were made to use this in death camps at Auschwitz and Majdanek.

CROSS-REFERENCE OPENING OF BELZEC: PAGES 18–19

Wannsee Conference

The villa at Wannsee, just outside Berlin, where high-ranking Nazis met on 20 January 1942 to coordinate the organization of the Holocaust.

Wannsee, a suburb of Berlin, was chosen as the place for a secret meeting of Nazis to discuss the organization of the final stage of the Holocaust. Poison gas had been decided upon as the most efficient means of killing, and new camps where the gassing would take place were being planned. It was now necessary to coordinate arrangements for the selection and transportation of Jews from across Europe to the death camps. This was the purpose of the Wannsee Conference.

DECISIONS AT WANNSEE

Himmler's deputy, Reinhard Heydrich, was in charge of the meeting and he began by presenting a list of the numbers of Jews still alive in various European countries. No one spoke of mass murder but everyone at the meeting knew what was meant when Heydrich referred to the 'Final Solution'. Europe, he explained, was 'to be combed through from west to east' for Jews who would then be

The camp system

Six death camps were created and they were all in Poland: Auschwitz, Belzec, Chelmno, Majdanek, Sobibor and Treblinka. Three of them – Auschwitz, Majdanek and Treblinka – were first built as labour and concentration camps for Jews and other groups that the Nazis wanted to isolate from society. There were also about fifty concentration camps and in many of them Jews were forced to work in extremely harsh conditions until they died. At Mauthausen concentration camp, the death rate for Jews reached a hundred per cent.

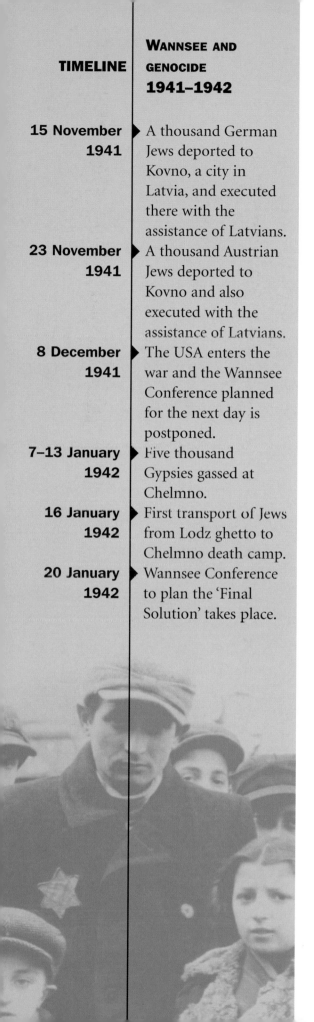

This map shows just a few of the many Nazi concentration camps that existed. Rail routes to Auschwitz made it the biggest of the six death camps.

transported 'farther to the East', meaning the death camps in Poland. Able-bodied Jews in good health would not be immediately murdered but used as slave labour. There was also a discussion about how to treat 'half-Jews' who, according to the Nuremberg Laws, were not completely Jewish.

ADOLF EICHMANN

The Wannsee Conference lasted less than a day and was conducted like a high-level business meeting. It was a very civilized affair, with lunch, drinks, and cigars provided for the fifteen men present, although the purpose of the conference was to plan genocide. The content of the meeting is known because the minutes (what was said) were written by one of the men present, an SS officer called Adolf Eichmann.

CROSS-REFERENCE AUSCHWITZ DEATH CAMP: PAGES 22–23

Belzec Death Camp Starts Operating

Jews in the ghetto at Lublin in Poland, which was situated very close to Majdanek, another of the death camps.

When it was realized that the methods of killing at Chelmno could not efficiently deal with the huge number of intended victims, it was decided to build fixed gas chambers. The first death camp to start operating with its own gas chamber was at Belzec and there, in less than a year, somewhere in the region of half a million Jews were killed. Of all the Jews deported to Belzec, only a handful are known to have survived.

PROCEDURES AT BELZEC

Like the death camps that came after it, Belzec was chosen as a site because it was close to a railway line and to an area where there were many Jews. As became common practice at most of the death camps, victims were told they were being transported to a place of work. Arriving at the camp, they were told to undress and hurried along by guards to what the victims were

told was a shower room. As at Chelmno, the poison gas was carbon monoxide and within about half an

A monstrous camp

'From everywhere comes the news about the incredible violence against the Jews. They are bringing trainloads of Jews from Czechoslovakia, Germany, and even from Belgium. They are also resettling the Jews ... and taking them somewhere towards Belzec. Today I heard a story about what they did to the Jews in Lublin. **It is difficult to believe it's true.** Today they deported Jews from Izbica – they were also taken to Belzec, where there is supposed to be some monstrous camp.'

Zygmunt Klukowski, a Polish doctor, recorded what he was hearing about Belzec in his diary, 26 March 1942.
Quoted in Dan Cohn-Sherbok, *Understanding the Holocaust* (Cassell, 1999).

MORE DEATH CAMPS 1942

March–April 1942 ▶ Death camps at Belzec, Sobibor and Majdanek start operating.

June 1942 ▶ Gas chambers at Auschwitz are made ready for operation.

July 1942 ▶ Death camp at Treblinka starts operating. The first deportation occurs on 22 July and by the end of the month over 66,000 Jews from Warsaw have been deported to Treblinka and killed.

hour everyone inside the gas chamber was dead. One of the few survivors described how, when it was over and the door opened, the dead were still standing 'like pillars … not having any space to fall.'

HISTORY OF BELZEC

There were three wooden gas chambers when the camp started operating on 17 March 1942. Later, these were replaced by six concrete-made chambers that could handle up to a thousand victims at a time. The trains that brought victims to Belzec travelled mostly at night. Lublin was the Polish city closest to Belzec and, by the end of 1942, all the Jews in this region had been killed. By this time, a far larger death camp at Auschwitz was in operation and so Belzec was closed down.

CROSS-REFERENCE
AUSCHWITZ DEATH CAMP: PAGES 22–23

The memorial at the site of the Belzec death camp, where around half a million victims of Nazism were murdered.

ZIEMIO, NIE KRYJ MOJEJ KRWI, IŻBY MÓJ KRZYK NIE USTAWAŁ. KSIĘG

EARTH, DO NOT COVER MY BLOOD; LET THERE BE NO RESTING PLACE FOR MY OUTCRY! JOB, 16:18

First Deportation of Jews from France

After most of Western Europe was conquered by Germany in 1940, Jewish communities in the region also became the victims of Nazism. Jews in German-occupied lands were rounded up for transportation to the death camps and to the many concentration and labour camps in Poland. In France, it was the French authorities who had the task of identifying Jews and rounding them up for the Nazis. The main holding camp was at Drancy, a suburb of Paris. Non-French Jews were the first to leave here in a train on 28 March 1942; their destination was Auschwitz in Poland. Over the next two years, just under 80,000 Jews were killed at Auschwitz as a result of deportations from France. This included 4,000 children whom the French authorities separated from their parents and sent to Auschwitz.

OTHER DEPORTATIONS

In the Netherlands, the main holding camp for Jews was near the town of Westerbork and from here trains left

Some of the children arrested in and around Paris in July 1942, before being deported to Auschwitz where they were likely to be gassed.

Jews in Italy

Italy joined the side of Germany in World War II and until 1943 the whole country was under the rule of a dictator. Anti-Semitism, however, was not a strong force in Italy and the Italians refused to deport its Jews. It was only in 1943, a month after the dictator was overthrown, that Germany invaded and began deporting Jews. As in France, it was the country's police force that assisted the Holocaust, and around 8,000 Italian Jews were killed in Auschwitz.

CROSS-REFERENCE
AUSCHWITZ DEATH
CAMP: PAGES
22–23

TIMELINE

DEPORTATIONS 1941–1944

20 May 1941 ▶ German announcement that no Jews can leave occupied territory, including France.

14 May–June 1941 ▶ The round-up of foreign-born Jews in France begins.

28 March 1942 ▶ First transportation of foreign-born Jews from France to Auschwitz.

14 July 1942 ▶ Jews begin to be rounded up in the Netherlands.

2 August 1942 ▶ First train of deported Jews leaves Belgium for a death camp.

October 1943 ▶ Jews first begin to be deported from Italy.

31 July 1944 ▶ Last train departs from Belgium for Auschwitz.

on a regular basis for Auschwitz. Over 100,000 Jews were deported and only a few thousand of these managed to survive. Around 34,000 Dutch Jews were also sent to the death camp at Sobibor and of these only 19 survived. Over 20,000 Jews in the Netherlands went into hiding during the Nazi occupation but some 8,000 of these were betrayed to the authorities and then deported.

It was a similar story in Belgium where over 25,000 Jews were deported; 5,000 of those who died were children under the age of sixteen. Sweden remained neutral in World War II and many Jews living in neighbouring Norway and Denmark were able to flee there and find safety.

DECEIVING THE VICTIMS

As happened in Poland, the Jews who were deported from Western Europe were told they were being resettled, that they would have new homes, and that they could bring a suitcase of personal belongings with them.

A Jewish family, arrested in Amsterdam where they lived, on their way to a train station for the journey to a death camp.

Himmler Visits Auschwitz

Most of the death camps were very small in size. Sobibor, which was not the smallest, occupied an area of only 600 metres by 400 metres. Nevertheless, in the three camps of Belzec, Sobibor and Treblinka a total of around 1.7 million people were murdered. There was still a need, though, for a larger killing centre and the largest of the death camps was established near the Polish town of Oswiecim – the German name of which is Auschwitz.

17 JULY 1942

THE AUSCHWITZ CAMPS

Auschwitz was first built as a prison work camp but, because it had railway links with other parts of Europe, it was selected as suitable for enlargement. A second camp was built some three kilometres away, near the village of Birkenau. It was here, at Auschwitz II, that large gas chambers were installed and it became the main killing centre for Europe's Jews. A third camp, Auschwitz III, was later added as a centre for slave labour and was run by a large German chemical company called I. G. Farben. In addition, over 20 smaller work camps run by various companies were established in the same area and the companies paid the Nazi government for the slave labour they employed. Auschwitz is the common name given to the three main camps and the various smaller ones.

HIMMLER'S VISIT

During an inspection tour in 1942, Himmler travelled around an area of 65 square kilometres, which would come under the control of Auschwitz. On 17 July he witnessed the arrival of a group of prisoners and their gassing and was very pleased with the efficiency of the operation. The plans for enlargement went ahead and, by the middle of 1943, there were four

Heinrich Himmler, who was in overall charge of organizing the Holocaust.

TIMELINE	**AUSCHWITZ AND TREBLINKA 1940–1942**
May 1940	▶ Building work on Auschwitz I prison camp begins.
1 March 1941	▶ Himmler makes his first visit to Auschwitz and announces plans for a three-fold expansion in the camp's holding capacity.
27 March 1941	▶ Auschwitz officials meet representatives from I. G. Farben to discuss their cooperation.
February 1942	▶ Building of Auschwitz II begins.
17 July 1942	▶ Himmler visits Auschwitz to witness the arrival and gassing of prisoners.
October 1942	▶ New gas chambers at Treblinka in operation.

gas chambers, each with their own crematorium. On arrival at Auschwitz, Jews were lined up and those considered not suitable for work went to the gas chambers while the others were sent to one of the work camps.

CROSS-REFERENCE AUSCHWITZ DEATH CAMP: PAGES 20–21, 38–39 BETRAYAL OF ANNE FRANK: PAGES 34–35

Replicas of the furnaces that were used in one part of Auschwitz to cremate the corpses of 70,000 victims between 1940 and 1943.

The *Sonderkommando*

Auschwitz was a death factory. To run it efficiently, the bodies of those gassed had to be removed quickly from the gas chamber and burnt so that the next group of victims could take their place.

Special groups of Jewish prisoners, called the *Sonderkommando*, had the task of opening the gas chambers and, using straps, dragging out the bodies for removal to a crematorium. Jewish dentists had the task of pulling out any gold teeth before the bodies were fed into a giant oven. Most members of the *Sonderkommando* were killed when they became too weak to carry on with their work.

Deportations from Warsaw Ghetto Begin

A group of Jews being led from the Warsaw ghetto, a photograph that was exhibited at the Nuremberg Trials.

Jewish councils, called the *Judenrat*, were responsible for managing day-to-day life in the ghettos and organizing teams of Jewish workers that the Nazis wanted to use. Members of a *Judenrat* had a lot of power and some of them abused their position by helping some Jews at the expense of others. While many families starved, others with valuables and money could survive by buying food on the black market. Walls or fences usually surrounded the ghettos and only the work teams were allowed out during the day.

WARSAW GHETTO

The Jewish area of Warsaw, the capital of Poland, became the largest ghetto

'Better to die with honour than to be gassed in Treblinka'

'Today every Jew should know the fate of those resettled. The same fate awaits the remaining few in Warsaw. The conclusion then is: Don't let yourself be caught! Hide, don't let yourself be taken away, **run away, don't be fooled** ... The dishonourable traitors and helpers – the Jewish police – should be boycotted! Don't believe them, beware of them. Stand up against them!'

A paper published by a resistance group in the Warsaw ghetto spells out the truth.
Quoted in Lucy S. Dawidowicz, *The War against the Jews* (Penguin, 1987).

CROSS-REFERENCE
UPRISING IN
WARSAW GHETTO:
PAGES 28–29
VILNA GHETTO:
PAGES 30–31

TIMELINE	THE GHETTOS 1940–1942
May 1940	First ghetto created in Poland, at Lodz, by the Nazis.
3 October 1940	German announcement that all Jews living outside Warsaw's Jewish district had to leave their homes and move into the area; non-Jewish Poles ordered to leave.
12 October 1940	Announcements by loudspeakers in Warsaw said that the ghetto had to be completed before the end of the month.
15 November 1940	Warsaw ghetto officially in existence and all Jews forbidden to leave the area; work begins on the building of walls around the ghetto.
28 July 1942	Group formed in the Warsaw ghetto to resist the Nazis.

with around half a million people forced to live there. When the Treblinka death camp was ready, the Warsaw *Judenrat* was ordered to organize and assemble 6,000 Jews for deportation each day. The excuse was that they were being moved further east in order to be 'resettled' and that each person could bring with them 15 kilograms of luggage and food for three days. A Jewish police force of a thousand helped organize the deportation but rumours of the death camps caused other Jews to organize a resistance group.

TREBLINKA DEATH CAMP

Between 22 July and early October 1942, over 300,000 Jews were taken from the Warsaw ghetto to Treblinka, where most of them died. Treblinka was a large death camp at which, in the summer of 1942, around 10,000 people were being gassed every day. A new commandant of the camp ordered that the hut beside the platform where Jews arrived by train should be disguised as a normal railway station to help deceive the victims. Signs for waiting rooms were erected and flowers were planted in tubs.

This man's job was to collect the bodies of fellow Jews who died from starvation or illness in the Warsaw ghetto.

Special Request for Transport

The invasion of the Soviet Union in 1941 did not go well for Germany. Although over 3 million Soviet citizens had been killed, and another 3 million taken prisoner, the Soviet Union had not been defeated. Hitler planned a final, knockout attack on the city of Stalingrad. Soldiers and supplies had to be moved eastwards to prepare for the attack but this was not allowed to interfere with the transportation of Jews to the death camps. Himmler's office was informed in July 1942 that a train with 5,000 Jews was leaving Warsaw every day for Treblinka and two trains a week were reaching Belzec with the same number of victims.

HIMMLER'S SPECIAL REQUEST

The attack on Stalingrad began in August 1942, but by the end of that year the German army was surrounded and close to surrender. The soldiers were surviving on food rations of less than 60 grams of bread a day and less than 15 grams of sugar. It was vital to move more supplies to the Soviet Union, so trains for non-military purposes were stopped.

Himmler, however, did not want the Holocaust to slow down. On 20 January 1943, he made a special request for more trains. His request was agreed to and trains once again began transporting Jews to the death camps from across all of Nazi-occupied Europe. Days later, the Germans surrendered at Stalingrad. It proved a turning point in World War II and, in this way, brought the possibility of an end to the Holocaust closer.

ORDINARY GERMANS AND THE HOLOCAUST

It took a great deal of planning and careful organization to transport thousands of Jews across Europe every day. It required people to sit in offices and work with train timetables and it needed the assistance of railway staff

Troops from the Soviet Union gathering near Stalingrad, ready for the attack on enemy forces that would lead to the surrender of the German army.

STALINGRAD 1942–1943

25 August 1942 ▶	Battle of Stalingrad begins.
31 August 1942 ▶	German forces, just 25 km outside Stalingrad, are halted by fierce resistance from the Soviet army.
3 September 1942 ▶	One division of the German army is within 8 km of the centre of Stalingrad.
18 October 1942 ▶	Soviet forces, having held their defences, begin some counter-moves against the Germans at Stalingrad.
23 November 1942 ▶	German army at Stalingrad begins to be surrounded by Soviet forces.
31 January 1943 ▶	German army south of Stalingrad surrenders.

as well as soldiers. After Jews had been gassed, their valuables were collected together and transported back to Germany. Historians do not agree on how much of this was known by ordinary Germans, but Jews were disappearing across Europe and rumours of what was happening to them must have reached some Germans. In the ghettos, many Jews came to realize that the trains were taking them away to be killed.

Jewish women from the Warsaw ghetto walking into one of the cattle-trucks that would take them to a death camp.

CROSS-REFERENCE
GERMAN INVASION OF THE SOVIET UNION: PAGES 12–13

Himmler's letter of 20 January 1943

'If I am to wind things up quickly, I must have more trains for transports. I know very well how taxing the situation is for the railways and what demands are constantly made of you. Just the same, I must make this request of you: Help me get more trains.'

Himmler's letter was to Theodor Ganzenmüller, the Head of Transportation in Germany.
Quoted in Lucy S. Dawidowics, *The War against the Jews 1933–45* (Penguin, 1987).

Uprising in the Warsaw Ghetto

By the end of summer 1942, around 60,000 Jews were left in the Warsaw ghetto and most of them knew it was only a matter of time before they also were sent to Treblinka. The ghetto's resistance group, which had been formed in the summer, made plans to defy any further attempts at deportation.

Planning resistance

The first act of defiance came in January 1943 when a small number of Jews fought German troops for three days before they were all killed. By April, after hearing rumours that the ghetto would be cleared of all remaining Jews, the resistance was better prepared. The available weapons – 2 machine guns, 17 rifles, about 500 pistols, and thousands of grenades and petrol bombs – were small in number compared to what the Germans had. Most of those prepared to fight knew they could not succeed but they still wanted to make a stand. They prepared shelters for the unarmed in the hope that in the confusion of battle some could escape through the sewers and reach the outskirts of the city.

The uprising

When the Germans entered the ghetto on 19 April, they were met by gunfire and grenades. When the Germans

German troops set fire to the Warsaw ghetto in their efforts to defeat the uprising taking place there.

Resistance in Auschwitz II

A group of women attacked their guards at Birkenau in 1943 rather than walk into a gas chamber. One of the women grabbed a gun from a guard, and shot two of them, while others used their bare hands to resist. All the women were eventually shot and the surname of only one of them, Horowitz, is now known.

In 1944, a group of *Sonderkommando* who were Greek Jews attacked their guards and set off explosives in one of the crematoria. The explosives had been smuggled to them by women working in a nearby munitions factory. These women were later discovered and tortured before being executed; all but three of the *Sonderkommando* were also executed.

CROSS-REFERENCE
VILNA GHETTO:
PAGES 30–31

TIMELINE

UPRISINGS 1943

16 May 1943 ▶ The Warsaw ghetto 'is no longer in existence' reports a German officer to his superiors.

21 May 1943 ▶ Armed resistance by Jews in the ghetto of Brody.

2 August 1943 ▶ Armed uprising in Treblinka death camp.

14 October 1943 ▶ Armed breakout of 300 people from Sobibor death camp.

realized how organized the resistance was, they began burning the ghetto. The uprising lasted for nearly a month and hundreds were killed and over 50,000 Jews were later deported. Ahron Karmi, one of those who managed to escape, found that life outside the ghetto was far from safe: 'After two years, from this group of eighty people who went out to the forest only eleven people were left.'

The Warsaw ghetto was largely destroyed in the uprising but in September the Germans sent in Polish labourers to demolish the remaining walls and buildings.

Frightened families are arrested and led out from the Warsaw ghetto after the uprising in January 1943.

Emptying the Vilna Ghetto

Around Poland's eastern borders, there were many armed Jewish resistance groups and the largest, named after the Bielski brothers, built its own settlement in an isolated forest in Belarus. The Bielski group sent members into ghettos to help guide people who wanted to escape. The group also killed those who betrayed Jews in hiding, hoping it would then be safer for those who had not yet been caught.

The Bielski brothers

Two brothers in the Bielski family refused to join their fellow Jews in a ghetto and escaped into a Belarus forest. In the summer of 1942, they found out that the rest of their family and many other relatives and friends had been murdered. They formed a resistance group of over thirty members and gradually built an organized movement. Towards the end of 1943, they established a permanent camp and accepted all Jews who wanted to join them. By 1944, when the Russians forced the Germans to withdraw, the Bielski brothers' group numbered 1,200.

BETRAYAL

There were also Jewish resistance groups in the forests outside Vilna in Lithuania; they offered to help rescue the Jews in the city's ghetto. Over 30,000 Jews in Vilna had already been killed and the remaining 20,000 were herded into the ghetto. A resistance group developed within the Vilna ghetto but the *Judenrat* wanted nothing to do with them and felt it was better to keep their heads down and wait for the end of the war.

When the Nazis demanded the handover of the ghetto's resistance leader, Yitzhak Wittenberg, the *Judenrat* betrayed him. Wittenberg was rescued but he gave himself up when the Nazis threatened to kill many in the ghetto. The resistance

Two Jewish children in Vilna, now the capital of Lithuania, where thousands of Jews were crowded into a ghetto after the German invasion of the Soviet Union.

group fled into the forest when the ghetto's other Jews refused to plan any kind of resistance. On 23 September 1943 the Nazis set about emptying the ghetto and some 20,000 Jews were transported to camps where most of them died.

BIALYSTOK GHETTO

In another large ghetto, Bialystok, there was also an armed resistance group. The *Judenrat* would not agree to an uprising while the majority of the ghetto's population was still alive. They continued to cooperate with the Nazis and organized the deportation of some of their fellow Jews, thinking that this was the only way if most were to survive.

When the Nazis unexpectedly announced that everyone would be deported, only a few resisted and died fighting. Over 30,000 Jews quietly got on trains that took them to two death camps.

CROSS-REFERENCE THE WARSAW GHETTO: PAGES 28–29

A memorial in the forest of Paneriai, now part of Lithuania, where more than 100,000 people, including 70,000 Jews, were executed between 1941 and 1944.

Rescue of Denmark's Jews

Danish people listen to an announcement informing them of the Nazi occupation of their country in 1940.

Denmark was conquered by Germany in 1940 but allowed to keep its own government in return for accepting Nazi power. By 1943, the retreat of German forces from the Soviet Union had encouraged Danish resistance. The Germans had now taken full control of Denmark and planned for the deportation of the country's 8,000 Jews. The round-up was due on 1 October 1943 but Danish politicians, who had discovered this a month earlier, passed on the news to groups resisting Nazism. The groups worked to save their fellow-citizens by organizing their escape in boats to neighbouring Sweden, a neutral country which offered refuge.

ORDINARY CITIZENS

On the morning of 2 October, fewer than 500 Jews had been captured by the Nazis. Those still in the country were in hiding and by the end of the month just over 7,000 had successfully escaped to Sweden. It required thousands of ordinary Danes and money contributed by all sections of society to make the operation successful. All those involved took a risk in helping Jews. The Danish government also worked hard to protect the 500 Jews who had been rounded up and, although imprisoned, the Jews were never sent to a death camp.

RESISTANCE IN BULGARIA

The people of Bulgaria also chose not to accept Nazi plans for the deportation of their country's Jews. A pro-Nazi government had been set up in Bulgaria, anti-Semitic measures were taken, and 11,000 Jews from Bulgarian-occupied territory were sent to death camps. When, however,

TIMELINE

BULGARIA AND DENMARK 1940–1943

February 1940 ▶ Pro-Nazi government established in Bulgaria.

April 1940 ▶ Denmark invaded by Germany.

January 1943 ▶ A high-ranking Nazi official arrives in Sofia, the capital of Bulgaria, to press for the deportation of the country's Jews.

22 February 1943 ▶ The Bulgarian government agrees to the deportation of Jews from the country.

24 May 1943 ▶ Protests in Bulgaria against the deportation of Jews.

1 October 1943 ▶ Round-up of Denmark's Jews begins; Danes organize a rescue mission.

plans were announced to deport the Jews who lived in Bulgaria there were many protests. Ordinary people chose to defend their fellow citizens; protesters threatened to lie on railway tracks to prevent the departure of deportation trains. As a result of public protest, the 48,000 Jews in Bulgaria remained there and, although imprisoned until the government was overthrown in 1944, survived and eventually returned to their homes.

There were no traditions of anti-Semitism within Denmark or Bulgaria, which helped save their Jews. As in Italy, Jews had been accepted into communities and ordinary people were prepared to defend them.

CROSS-REFERENCE ▶
DEPORTATIONS IN OTHER COUNTRIES: PAGES 20–21

Crowds in Sofia, the capital of Bulgaria, celebrate the liberation of their country by troops from the Soviet Union in 1944.

Defying the deportations

'Take your stand in front of your Jewish neighbours' homes and don't let them be led away by force! **Hide their children** and do not hand them over to the executioners! Crowd the Jewish quarters and demonstrate your solidarity with the oppressed Jews.'

An appeal to citizens by an anti-Nazi group in Bulgaria, in February 1943. Quoted in Martin Gilbert, *Never Again* (HarperCollins, 2000).

Anne Frank Betrayed

When Jews were being rounded up for deportation to a ghetto or a camp, some managed to hide with the assistance of non-Jewish people. This is what happened in the case of the Franks, a Jewish family who had fled to the Netherlands to escape persecution in Germany.

THE DIARY

With the German invasion of the Netherlands, the Franks once again found themselves at the mercy of Nazism. The family prepared a hiding place in an empty building, which they moved into in July 1942, and four Dutch helpers brought them food and clothing. One of the family, Anne, kept a diary throughout the period of her hiding. The diary was a present from her father on her thirteenth birthday. The teenager addressed her diary to an imaginary friend, Kitty: 'I hope I shall be able to confide in you completely, as I have never been able to do in anyone before and I hope you will be a great support and comfort to me.'

BETRAYAL

The family survived for two years before being betrayed and arrested on 4 August 1944. In 1944, the German army was retreating from Allied forces that had landed in northern France, but deportation trains to Auschwitz were still being planned. The Frank family was put on the last train leaving the Netherlands. At Auschwitz the family was split up and over the following months Anne, and all of her family except her father, were killed or died in various camps. Anne was moved with her sister, Margot, to the Bergen-Belsen concentration camp in Germany. Margot died of typhus around the end of February 1945, and Anne died a few days later.

A photograph of Anne Frank, taken before she and her family went into hiding from the Nazis in Amsterdam.

ANNE FRANK
1929–1945

12 June 1929	Anne Frank is born in Germany.
June 1942	Anne Frank receives a diary for her thirteenth birthday.
6 July 1942	Frank family move into their hiding place in Amsterdam.
4 August 1944	Frank family betrayed and arrested.
8 August 1944	Frank family moved to a transit camp at Westerbork.
3 September 1944	Frank family deported to Auschwitz.
6 October 1944	Anne and her sister Margot moved to Bergen-Belsen concentration camp.
February–March 1945	Anne and Margot die at Bergen-Belsen.

Otto Frank, the father of Anne, survived the Holocaust and lived to show a visitor the entrance to his family's hiding place on the fiftieth anniversary of Anne's birth.

THE DIARY SURVIVES

Anne's diary was found by one of the family's Dutch helpers. In this way, it survived the war and was later published.

CROSS-REFERENCE DEPORTATIONS OF JEWS: PAGES 20–21, 32–33

'We must clench our teeth'

'Would the long-awaited liberation that has been talked of so much, but which still seems too wonderful, **too much like a fairy-tale**, ever come true? Could we be granted victory this year, 1944? We don't know yet, but hope is revived within us; it gives us fresh courage, and makes us strong again… Now more than ever we must clench our teeth and not cry out. France, Russia, Italy, and Germany, too, can all cry out and give vent to their misery, but we haven't the right to do that yet!'

This is part of Anne Frank's entry in her diary for 6 June 1944, after hearing of the Allied invasion.
Anne Frank, *The Diary of Anne Frank* (Puffin Books, 2002).

Deportations from Hungary Resume

A Jewish couple in the Budapest ghetto, wearing the yellow stars they were ordered to display. They are likely to have died in the Holocaust.

Hungary had a population of over 750,000 Jews when Hitler decided in 1944 to send in an army and take over the country. Ghettos were created so that Jews could be rounded up for deportation to Auschwitz. The majority of Hungarian Jews were sent to the gas chambers and the killing was so well organized that over 320,000 Jews were murdered in less than two months.

A TEMPORARY INTERRUPTION

In July 1944, international efforts were made to save the country's remaining Jews, and the leader of the Hungarian government stopped the deportations. Officials in Hungary, representing Sweden, Italy and Switzerland, also began issuing as many travel documents as they could in order to provide a safe journey out of the country for thousands of Jews. In October, however, Hungarian Nazis took control of the government and the round-up of Jews carried on. Approximately 80,000 were made ready for their deportation to begin on 1 November.

Tricking the prisoners

'The SS men would warn them, "Please remember the number of your hanger for the clothes. Tie both shoes well, and put your clothing in one pile, because **they will be handed back to you at the end of the showers**."'

Yehuda Bakon, a Hungarian, recalls the attempt to deceive Jews being asked to undress before entering one of the gas chambers at Auschwitz.
Quoted in Martin Gilbert, *Never Again* (HarperCollins, 2000).

TIMELINE

HUNGARY 1944–1945

18 March 1944 ▶ German occupation of Hungary.

19 March 1944 ▶ Two hundred Jews arrested in Budapest, capital of Hungary, and deported.

29 April 1944 ▶ First deportations from Hungary to Auschwitz.

6 June 1944 ▶ D-Day landings in northern France and troops move eastward, advancing on German forces.

17 January 1945 ▶ Soviet soldiers enter Warsaw.

14 February 1945 ▶ Soviet soldiers enter Budapest.

22 April 1945 ▶ Soviet Union launches final assault against Berlin.

DEPORTATIONS CONTINUE

By this time, towards the end of 1944, Soviet forces were advancing across eastern Europe towards Germany. At the same time, American, British and other forces were advancing westward from France. Germany was being squeezed from both sides and was close to defeat. The rounded-up Jews in Hungary were to be used as slave labour in factories in Germany as part of a last-ditch attempt to avoid total defeat. This time there were no trains available for transport, so the Jews were forced to set off on foot on a march of over 150 kilometres. Food was not provided, it was wintertime, and thousands died or were shot along the way.

There were still over 100,000 Jews in the Hungarian capital and they suffered greatly over the winter of 1944. Many died, but the war was coming to an end and those who survived did not face deportation.

A scene on the railway ramp at the Auschwitz death camp as Hungarian Jews are divided into the able bodied, on the left, and the others, on the right, who have been selected for immediate gassing.

CROSS-REFERENCE THE HOLOCAUST CONTINUES: PAGES 40–41

Liberation of Auschwitz

The entrance gate and guardhouse at Auschwitz. After the war, Allied troops brought groups of German citizens to the camp to make them see what had taken place behind the entrance.

As Soviet forces advanced westward towards Germany, it became clear that they would soon reach the death camps in Poland. The SS made plans to dismantle and remove the gas chambers and other equipment so that no evidence remained of what had taken place. Many Jews still alive at the camps were hastily killed – in one week in November 1943 some 50,000 Jews were executed at Majdanek in front of ditches near the gas chambers.

The scene at Treblinka

When Treblinka camp was liberated, the scene was described by a witness, Dr Adolf Berman: 'I saw a sight I shall never forget, a tremendous area of many kilometres, and all over this area were scattered skulls, bones – tens of thousands; and piles of shoes – among them tens of thousands of little shoes.'

Auschwitz liberated

The Holocaust continued at Auschwitz because the Nazis wanted to kill all the Hungarian Jews. The last gassing at Auschwitz took place in October 1944 and the dismantling of the equipment began shortly afterwards. The camp network at Auschwitz, however, was so large that all had not been destroyed by the time Soviet soldiers arrived on 27 January 1945. The soldiers found the area where victims' personal belongings were stored and were astonished to discover 38,000 pairs of shoes and hundreds of thousands of women's clothes and men's suits.

By this time, most of the remaining Jews had been forced to leave Auschwitz and march to work camps in Germany. Some, though, were left behind alive. In January 1945, these survivors – 600 prisoners in a slave

TIMELINE	**END OF THE CAMPS 1942–1945**
December 1942	▶ Closure of Belzec death camp
November 1943	▶ Closure of Sobibor death camp.
December 1943	▶ Closure of Treblinka death camp.
July 1944	▶ Soviet army reaches Majdanek death camp.
January 1945	▶ Closure of Chelmno death camp.
18 January 1945	▶ Forced march out of Auschwitz begins.

labour camp – saw Soviet soldiers dressed in white camouflage suits and realized the camp had been finally liberated. Eva Mozes Kor was ten years old at the time and remembered the scene: 'We ran up to them and they gave us hugs, cookies and chocolates. Being so alone, a hug meant more than anybody could imagine because that replaced the human worth we were starving for.' The liberation of Auschwitz was not highly publicized at the time, partly because it was Soviet, not British or American, troops who first arrived there.

CROSS-REFERENCE
AUSCHWITZ: PAGES 22–23
THE HOLOCAUST CONTINUES: PAGES 40–41

A collection of shoes, belonging to victims at Auschwitz, that the Nazis left behind when they abandoned the camp in 1945.

The human cost

In total, around 1.25 million people were murdered at Auschwitz and nine out of every ten victims were Jews. The largest group came from Hungary (438,000), followed by Poland (300,000), then France (69,114), the Netherlands (60,085) and Greece (55,000). Smaller numbers came from other European countries. Around 70,000 political prisoners from Poland and 10,000 Soviet prisoners of war were also killed. The Nazis wanted to eliminate some non-Jewish groups too – over 20,000 Gypsies, as well as unknown numbers of homosexuals, also died at Auschwitz.

Jews Shot on Death March

Although the death camps had stopped operating by the end of 1944, this did not bring the Holocaust to an end. It continued as Jews held as slave labourers were forced to move from the work camps across Poland. These journeys usually began on foot, before the Jews were packed into railway cattle-trucks. So many people died, these journeys become known as the death marches.

Auschwitz death march

The largest death march was made up of 60,000 prisoners from the various work camps at Auschwitz. As with the march of Hungarian Jews, it was winter, and food and proper clothing were not provided. Helena Citrónová, a survivor of the march from Auschwitz, described how she was unable to help other prisoners who 'dropped in the snow. They didn't have any strength left and they died. Each person took care of himself. Total chaos. Whoever lived – lived. Whoever died – died.'

Of those who did survive the march, many thousands later died because of the conditions in the German camps where they were deposited. There was little food and no medical attention, and when Allied soldiers reached camps like Bergen-Belsen, Buchenwald, Dachau and Mauthausen they were shocked at what they found.

After the liberation of the Bergen-Belsen camp by the Allies, German soldiers are made to bury the thousands who continued to die from starvation and disease as a result of their imprisonment.

'I watched them die'

'The state of their minds is plainly written on their faces, as **starvation has reduced their bodies to skeletons**... They are Jews and are dying now at the rate of three hundred a day. They must die and nothing can save them ... they crawl or totter out into the sunshine to die. I watched them make their last feeble journeys, and even as I watched they die.'

Peter Coombs, a British soldier at Belsen, writing to his wife about what he saw.
Quoted in Martin Gilbert, *Never Again* (HarperCollins, 2000).

CROSS-REFERENCE: DEATH MARCH FROM HUNGARY: PAGES 36–37

TIMELINE

HOLOCAUST CONTINUES 1945

18 January 1945 ▶ Start of death march from Auschwitz.

23 January 1945 ▶ Around a thousand Jewish women are forced to march westwards from a camp at Neusalz; only 200 survive the march that lasts 42 day and they are sent to the Bergen-Belsen camp.

13 April 1945 ▶ Allied troops enter Bergen-Belsen camp.

29 April 1945 ▶ Allied soldiers enter the Dachau camp.

The scene at Bergen-Belsen, where camp prisoners and death-march survivors looked like walking skeletons, was captured on film and shown worldwide. For many people this was their first awareness of the Holocaust, even though Bergen-Belsen itself was not a death camp.

THE END OF WAR DRAWS NEAR

By the beginning of April 1945, Soviet troops from the east and Americans from the west were close to meeting each other in Germany. In Berlin, Hitler committed suicide on 30 April as Soviet soldiers approached the German parliament building. On the same day, nearly 3,000 Jews were being marched from near Buchenwald to another camp when an Allied air raid presented them with a chance to escape. A thousand of them were caught and shot.

Prisoners in the Dachau concentration camp celebrate their freedom after the arrival of American troops in April 1945.

Opening Day of Nuremberg Trials

Two years before World War II came to an end, the Allied governments of the USA, the Soviet Union, and Britain declared that they would seek to put their enemies on trial for war crimes. Some British and American leaders thought it would be best if Nazi leaders were quickly executed, arguing that the legal grounds for a trial were not well established. In the end, though, it was decided to

Rudolf Hoess, the commandant of Auschwitz who believed he had nothing to feel guilty about, after his arrest for war crimes.

create a new International Military Tribunal to organize public trials.

ESCAPING JUSTICE

The trials of Nazi leaders began on 20 November 1945 in Nuremberg, the city where the anti-Semitic laws of 1935 were passed. Over twenty men were charged with war crimes and all but three were found guilty.

Only leading Nazis appeared at Nuremberg and many thousands of individuals who carried out the Holocaust escaped justice. Some 6,500 members of the SS who worked at Auschwitz survived the war but only around one in ten of these ever received any punishment for what they did. The most common defence, as used by some of those on trial in

Obeying orders

The man in charge of Auschwitz, Rudolf Hoess, was asked this question at his trial in Nuremberg:

'And it never occurred to you to refuse the orders that Himmler gave you regarding the so-called Final Solution?'

'No … I naturally had to obey orders.'

Josef Kramer, who took part in gassings at Auschwitz and later was in charge of Belsen camp, said the same at his trial:

'**I had no feelings** in carrying out these things, because I received an order.'

Quoted in Laurence Rees, *Auschwitz* (BBC Books, 2005) and Martin Gilbert, *Never Again* (HarperCollins, 2000).

CROSS-REFERENCE
NUREMBERG LAWS:
PAGES 8–9

TIMELINE

TRIALS OF NAZIS 1944–2001

27 November 1944
> Six SS guards from Majdanek death camp put on trial by Polish authorities.

7 May 1945
> Germany surrenders and the war in Europe comes to an end.

23 May 1945
> Himmler, head of the SS, commits suicide.

16 October 1946
> Execution of 12 Nazis found guilty at Nuremberg.

3 April 2001
> An SS officer who killed seven Jews in the last days of the war is sentenced to 12 years in jail.

Nuremberg, was that they were acting under orders and could not disobey. This argument was not accepted at Nuremberg and the legal principle was established that this is not an acceptable excuse for war crimes.

Rudolf Hoess, the Nazi who lived with his family at Auschwitz and managed the death camp, returned there in April 1947. He had been found guilty at Nuremberg and sentenced to death. He was executed at Auschwitz.

OTHER TRIALS

Poland and other countries in Eastern Europe conducted their own trials of Nazis involved in the Holocaust. In 1946, a British military court put on trial the owner and manager of the German company that manufactured the poison gas Zyklon B used at Auschwitz and other death camps. Trials of other Nazis have taken place over the years and a trial in 2001 was probably the last.

Two rows of Nazis on trial for war crimes at Nuremberg, sitting behind two rows of court officials.

Holocaust Denial Condemned in Court

The Holocaust came to an end with the defeat of Germany in World War II but this did not bring anti-Semitism to an end. Sometimes anti-Semitism takes the form of denying the Nazi genocide, claiming that the gas chambers were not used in the way they were and that, although many Jews were killed, Hitler himself had no knowledge of it.

DENYING THE HOLOCAUST

The author David Irving became briefly famous in 2000 when he sued the writer and publisher of a book that said he denied the Holocaust. The case attracted a lot of attention and members of the British National Party were in court to support Irving. He claimed that Auschwitz was only a work camp and that the gas chambers were used to de-louse corpses and objects. Survivors of Auschwitz appeared as witnesses to show that he was wrong and there was evidence from SS officers who saw gassings take place. Historians with expert knowledge of Nazism appeared in court to testify that Hitler knew very well that the Holocaust was taking place. The judge's verdict was given on 11 April and he declared that Irving was indeed a 'Holocaust denier'.

HOLOCAUST DENIAL TODAY

Holocaust denial has been adopted by small racist groups, known as the far

right, in many countries, including Britain, the USA, Germany and France. In the Middle East, Israel's treatment of Palestinians causes so much bitterness that it has lead to

A gravestone in a Jewish cemetery vandalized with a swastika by anti-Semites.

Evidence

'Dear finder, search everywhere, in every inch of soil. Dozens of documents are buried under it, mine and those of other persons, which will throw light on everything that was happening here. Great quantities of teeth are also buried here. It was we, the Kommando workers, who expressly have strewn them all over the terrain as many as could, so that the world should find material **traces of the millions of murdered people**.'

A note written and buried by a *Sonderkommando* at Auschwitz who realized the importance of evidence. Quoted in Martin Gilbert, *Never Again* (HarperCollins, 2000).

HOLOCAUST DENIAL 1978–2006

December 1978 and January 1979 ▶ Robert Faurisson, a professor at the University of Lyon in France, publishes letters in a national newspaper claiming that the Nazi gas chambers did not exist.

11 January 2000 ▶ The Irving trial opens in London.

11 April 2000 ▶ Irving loses libel case.

13 December 2005 ▶ President of Iran denies that the Holocaust occurred.

19 February 2006 ▶ Irving sentenced to three years in prison by an Austrian court for denying the Holocaust. He was released in December 2006 and put on probation.

anti-Semitism, with the government of Iran claiming that the Holocaust never happened. In Austria, where Hitler was born and where he learnt to be racist, it is illegal to deny the Holocaust. Racism was one of the roots of the Holocaust, so opposing racism is one important way of trying to prevent anything like the Holocaust happening again.

A group pleased to display their support for the Nazis march in Idaho in the USA.

Key Figures in the Holocaust

TUVIA BIELSKI (1906–1987)

Tuvia Bielski and his brothers were born into a poor Jewish farming family in Eastern Europe, then part of the Soviet Union. They refused to enter a ghetto and left home but their parents and two other brothers were murdered by the Nazis. The surviving three brothers formed a resistance group to fight the Germans and by the late summer of 1942 they had over thirty followers. Tuvia Bielski was appointed leader. At first, the group kept on the move but by the end of 1943 they had a permanent camp in a remote forest. Any Jewish refugees who wanted to join were accepted. By the summer of 1944, by which time the Soviet army had liberated their area, the Bielski group numbered over 1,200. The three brothers and their followers had created the largest armed resistance group dedicated to the rescue of Jews in Nazi-occupied Europe.

ANNE FRANK (1929–1945)

Anne Frank was born in Germany on 12 June 1929 but before the age of five she moved with her family to the Netherlands to escape persecution in Nazi Germany. She learnt to speak Dutch and had a happy childhood until May 1940 when the Germans invaded the Netherlands and the Frank family once more came under Nazi rule. She remained in hiding with the family until August 1944, when she was moved to a prison camp in the Netherlands, and on the 3 September she was one of those placed on the last deportation train from the Netherlands to Auschwitz. In October she was moved to the Bergen-Belsen concentration camp in Germany, where she died in March 1945.

REINHARD HEYDRICH (1904–1942)

Heydrich was Himmler's deputy and he played a leading part in the Holocaust. He joined the Nazi party in 1931 and then the SS. He organized the herding of Polish Jews into ghettos and the building of the death camps. He was in charge of the Wannsee Conference in January 1942 and four months later was assassinated by a resistance group. In revenge, Hitler ordered the destruction of a village thought to be associated with the resistance group. The village was burnt to the ground, all the men killed, the women sent to camps and the children removed to German families.

HEINRICH HIMMLER (1900–1945)

Himmler joined the Nazi party in 1925 and four years later was made head of Hitler's bodyguards, the SS. Himmler turned the SS into a powerful force and used it to carry out the Holocaust. He was also the head of a secret police force called the Gestapo. He was captured by the Allies in 1945 and committed suicide when he realized he could not make a deal with them.

ADOLF HITLER (1889–1945)

Hitler, born in Austria, moved to Germany as a young man and joined a small political party in 1919. This became the anti-Semitic Nazi party, which in the late 1920s expanded in size and importance. After 1933, when Hitler was made chancellor of Germany, the Nazis established themselves as dictators and put into practice their anti-Semitic ideas. He committed suicide in 1945 when Russian soldiers were only a few hundred metres away from his underground air-raid shelter in Berlin.

RUDOLF HOESS (1900–1947)

Hoess, believing in the existence of an international Jewish conspiracy as described in the *Protocols of the Elders of Zion*, joined the Nazi party as a young man. By joining the Nazis, as he explained in an autobiography written in prison awaiting execution for war crimes: 'Jewish supremacy would therefore be destroyed.' Hoess joined the SS and after six years of service, at the age of 39, he was appointed commandant of what was to become a concentration camp at Auschwitz. The camp had not yet been built and Hoess supervised its construction. In 1943, he was appointed overall commander of the SS at Auschwitz and was responsible for the smooth operation of the murder of Hungarian Jews.

Glossary

Allies countries at war against Germany in World War II
anti-Semitism racial prejudice against Jews
British National Party a small party in Britain opposed to non-white immigration; regarded mostly as racist
commandant the commanding officer in charge
concentration camps large prison camps where prisoners were forced to work under very harsh conditions and where many died
crematorium places where corpses are disposed of by burning
death camps camps where prisoners were systematically murdered
death march forced marching out and removal of prisoners from camps by the Nazis in the closing months of World War II
deportation process of removing people from their home or country
Einsatzgruppen special killing squad organized by the Nazis
far right term for extreme groups that often express racist attitudes
'Final Solution' Nazi term for their planned murder of all European Jews
genocide deliberate killing of a people or nation
ghetto town districts where Nazis forced Jews to live and from where they were later transported to death camps
Holocaust term used to refer to the Nazi-led murder of six million Jews in Europe
Judenrat German for 'Jewish Council' – groups established by the Nazis to help run the ghettos
pogrom anti-Jewish riots (organized or spontaneous)
protocols set of rules laying down how a group will behave
racist someone who believes that some races are better than others
Sonderkommando small groups established by the SS to lead people to the gas chambers and then dispose of the bodies
SS Nazi force that organized and ran the death camps
swastika ancient symbol which the Nazis adopted as their emblem
war crimes crimes committed by soldiers or politicians during a war
Zion hill of Jerusalem, which has become a name for the Jewish people or their religion

Further Information

BOOKS

Livia Britton-Jackson, *I Have Lived a Thousand Years* (Aladdin Books, 1999)
Clive A. Lawton, *Auschwitz: Story of a Nazi Death Camp* (Franklin Watts, 2002)
Pat Levy, *Questioning History: The Holocaust* (Hodder Wayland, 2003)
Pat Levy, *The Holocaust: Causes* (Hodder Wayland, 2000)
Sean Sheehan, *The Holocaust: The Death Camps* (Hodder Wayland, 2001)
Sean Sheehan, *How Did it Happen? The Holocaust* (Franklin Watts, 2005)

FIRST-HAND ACCOUNTS

Anne Frank, *The Diary of a Young Girl* (Puffin, 2002)

FILMS

Life is Beautiful
– the fictional story of a father who tries to protect his son from the horrors of the Holocaust
Schindler's List
– the true story of a German factory-owner who saves the lives of over a thousand Jews
The Pianist
– based on the memoirs of a survivor of the Krakow ghetto, who escaped transportation to a concentration camp

WEBSITES

www.bethshalom.com
– the website of the Holocaust Memorial and Education Centre
www.holocaust.about.com/education/holocaust
– photographs and information on Anne Frank and the death camps
www.remember.org
– explore the Holocaust through paintings, photographs, sculptures and remembrances

PLACES TO VISIT

The Holocaust Exhibition, Imperial War Museum, Lambeth Rd, London SE1 6HZ. Tel: 020 7416 5320.
– the exhibition is not recommended for children under the age of 14
The Holocaust Centre, Beth Shalom, Laxton, Newark, Nottingham NG22 OPA. Tel: 01623 83662

Index